Seasons

Desert Sketches

Seasons

Desert Sketches

by Ellen Meloy

Foreword by Annie Proulx

TORREY HOUSE PRESS

SALT LAKE CITY • TORREY

First Torrey House Press Edition, April 2019
Copyright © 2019 by Mark Meloy

Published by Torrey House Press
Salt Lake City, Utah
www.torreyhouse.org

International Standard Book Number: 978-1-948814-01-0
E-book ISBN: 978-1-948814-02-7
Audiobook ISBN: 978-1-948814-07-2
Library of Congress Control Number: 2018951996

Illustrations by Ellen Meloy
Cover design by Kathleen Metcalf
Interior design by Rachel Davis
Distributed to the trade by Consortium Book Sales and Distribution

This book produced in collaboration with KUER RadioWest

*To all who see clearly
and are unafraid to speak and write*

Contents

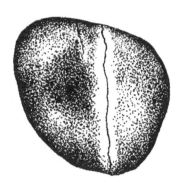

Introduction

One of Ellen Meloy's obituaries said her days of wandering began in the dry foothills of California. She left the desert for many years, following her father's work for the federal government. Ellen graduated from high school in London. She studied in Florence and Rome and at the Sorbonne in Paris. She worked as an illustrator and as an art curator in Baltimore and San Francisco.

Most of us came to know Ellen when the desert reclaimed her in Utah. She and her husband Mark made the tiny town of Bluff their home. In the really important ways, she never ever distinguished herself from all the other settlers of the West. Ellen said most people come to the desert for something else and then they strip themselves of everything but water and their thoughts. At some point, she said she crossed that threshold of absence in the desert. She looked beyond the austerity and found the place packed. Maybe that's when she started writing.

I met Ellen when she wrote essays in the 1990s for our radio station, KUER, an NPR affiliate in Salt Lake City. She would make the drive up north every so often to read a new batch. They were funny and beautiful and almost always surprising. But after she died in 2004, those tapes just sat there on a shelf. And we realized that was a shame. So, we decided to share them. I'm sure Ellen would resist the attempt to corral those stories into a theme, so we've simply organized them into the seasons of the years she spent in that desert and left it at that.

She would probably tell you to read them in any order you want, so do that. Think of these pages as a discovery you made of someone sassy and wise who died before her time.

Doug Fabrizio
Salt Lake City, Utah

Foreword

Naturalist and environmental writer Ellen Meloy, who died in 2004, loved the huge red rocks of the Four Corners region where Utah, Colorado, New Mexico, and Arizona come together in a dusty knot, a region of Navajo and Hopi languages and cultures with some of the most profound land views in North America. Her witty, freewheeling essays on the imbalance between humans and nature lightened up the Cassandra genre known as "environmental literature." Verlyn Klinkenborg, in an obituary remembrance, quoted her as saying that much nature writing ". . . sounds like a cross between a chloroform stupor and a high Mass."[1] She had the rare gift of seeing humor in the wild world and in our attempts to know it. She was a master of the telling phrase as when she described her place as "a tiny town in a land that looks like red bones" and commercial airliners as "flying culverts." She gave advice about toads: that we should not carry

---

[1] https://www.nytimes.com/2004/11/11/opinion/ellen-meloy.html

them around and "When you think about licking them, change your mind." She was curious about all landscapes and told her readers that when they were in new country they should pay attention and "ask why people call their landscape home, what they love or fear, what is blessed, what is destroyed." She often urged her readers and listeners to understand their biological addresses, to count the local wildlife, animals, birds, and plants as neighbors. The twitches of weather and climate were important to her and she wanted us to observe and make notes of what was happening in our backyard worlds as William Bartram or Thoreau did. For years in the 1850s Thoreau noted the blossoming times of wildflowers around Concord in his now-famous journals. Today's scientists used his meticulous data as evidence of climate change.[2]

Several of Meloy's essays were instant classics. "Lawn" condenses everything into two fierce sentences: "Throw massive amounts of water and petrochemicals on your grassy plot, let it push up from the soil, then cut it down to nubs before it can grow up and have sex and go to seed. A lawn is an endless cycle of doomed ecology." "Tourists in the Wild" lampoons New Yorkers lost in the terrifying Great West with a reference to bears, which we all know are spaced about twenty feet apart from the left side of the Rockies to the Pacific Ocean.

But her essays were not all wit and amusement. Some of the essays are less than benign, as "California" with its acid takeoff on the provocative bumper sticker "I'd rather be hunting and gathering" pasted on a

---

[2] Richard B. Primack, *Walden Warming*, U. Chicago Press, 2014.

luxe-mobile, or "Cracking Up" with its call to "small acts of defiance . . . against a suffocating culture of meaninglessness." And she could fire off hard truths dipped in sarcasm, as in "Animal News," which works up from an unnamed man's statement that wolves should not be reintroduced in the West because, as he says pejoratively, "The wolf kills for a living," to her point that we are "so estranged" from the lives of wild creatures that we offer them the choice of only living lives that suit us or dropping dead. Humans also are animals, she says—face it.

Some of the essays seem to have been written last week, so fresh are the topics. In November of 1996 Ellen Meloy was utterly sick of election jabber, of the inescapable faces on television and the incessant brainless repetitive rhetoric. "What," she says, "has become of the honorable and decent public servant? You won't find one in either political party, so kill your television." And she turns hers off. One of her finest essays, "Bluff," is about guns. The subject becomes important when "three anti-government extremists" who have killed a policeman in Colorado turn up not far from the Meloy place. Roadblocks, canine units, sheriffs and cops, and SWAT teams are everywhere. Her husband Mark has an old shotgun, but Ellen Meloy, who describes herself as a "token, squishy, white doughball of liberalism who still believed that if you hated government, maybe you should do something really radical to change things, like vote," does not have a gun. Readers! Let that sink in. She lives in the West, the American West, and does not have a gun! Yet lives to tell about it.

In the end, what we take away from the essays of Ellen Meloy is her impassioned request to us all to regard what is around us. "Pay attention to the weather, to what breaks your heart, to what lifts your heart. Write it down."

Amen, amen.

Annie Proulx
Port Townsend, Washington

Spring

·FEATHER·

I Stapled
My Hair to the Roof

I have just stapled my hair to the roof. I was unfurling heavy rolls of black felt over the pitched roof. Then I would lean in and staple the felt in place with tin caps. This requires grunt labor more than skill. But I was daydreaming about snowy egrets and leaned too far.

I'm my own boss. I'm in no particular rush. The day is so clear you could bite it. It seems a good time to enjoy the view and contemplate the dazzling spectacle of women awakening to their own full powers. With a slight twist I lie on my back.

Now, I will give you my precise location and concentric geography. The roof covers a modest owner-built home on eight acres of desert. Our house, me affixed to its south flank, faces a sheer escarpment of rose and beige sandstone. Below the cliff flows the San Juan River. Several miles southwest of my feet lies Monument Valley on the Navajo reservation. It's the home of the Mirage People, so called because it doesn't rain there often. House, river, the rez, Colorado Plateau, Utah, America, the world, the universe.

Stapled to the roof, I have serious thoughts about human potential. My Navajo neighbors have lived for centuries in a matrilineal society. In pioneer times, while the men mumbled about posses and punched each other's lights out, the grandmothers of my Anglo neighbors simply got off their horses and took care of business. Rural women could always raise roofs and corn, kids and hell. Yet today, one speaks of women marching into equality as if that were a different country. "No," I think as two turkey vultures circle above me, "we're simply occupying the rest of what has always been home." House, town, country, the world, the universe.

The turkey vultures don't see this geography of possibility. They see me, an edible, two-legged smudge on a plywood platter. I extricate my hair and return to felt and staple gun. Before I finish, two parties pass by on the highway. They pull over and watch, then offer me jobs. But I only have one roof in me, my own, and what I'd really like to do next is to run a tractor or a government. Perhaps a particle accelerator.

May 24, 1996

Animal News

Tonight's news was animal news. Once again I have timed dinner with a graphic wildlife documentary. Last night, forty hunger-crazed hyenas eviscerated a wildebeest, just as I lifted a fork load of cheesy lasagna to my mouth.

Tonight a man spoke against reintroducing wolves in the West. "The wolf kills for a living," he said. "I wonder if people who want wolves back would be so enthusiastic if they actually saw a wolf pack jump on some deer and eat that animal alive." He's right, I thought, pushing my plate aside, nature is rude and wolves should change their ways.

First, they should dump that disgusting pack technique and hire someone to procure their food. Next, they should sit up and use forks like the rest of us. Consign a few picnic tables to wolf packs, hand out bibs and moose liver, no longer pulsating of course. And while we're at it make them wear pants, so no family from Iowa has to suffer the sight of a rangy pack of buck-naked canids gnawing elk legs twenty yards from a souvenir shop.

Perhaps I'm overreacting. Every so often wild animals are ambushed by a rash of anthropocentric dodiness. In our confusion about nature's ways, we end up taking it out on the creatures themselves. In a national forest recently a bear was mistaken for a large rock and set ablaze when firefighters lit a backfire.

Elsewhere forest rangers were improving moose habitat by using dynamite to create boggy areas. They set off their charges just as two moose sauntered into the blasting site. Because of the force of the explosion, the meat could not be salvaged, they reported.

Westerners live closer to wildlife than most people. When we see an elk we know if it is right side up. We know the difference between a coyote and a poodle. So why suffer these outbreaks of animal anxiety? Perhaps the sight of natural predation, wolves bringing down an elk and eating it with the teeth they were born with, triggers the uneasy revelation that humans are animals.

Perhaps we pick on other creatures because we know we can be quite beastly ourselves. The ways of wild food are so remote from our minds we forget that we too are part of the feast. We're the executioner. Sometimes we're the entrée. Just ask a grizzly bear or a shark. Less and less we are the witness. So estranged are we from wild animals on their own terms, we insist they live on ours or be gone.

We may stalk our prey in the aisles of Safeway. We may wear pants at the dinner table, but we kill to live.

By making wolves into demons and bears into bonfires, we make ourselves into gods. We forget we are mammals. This is a dangerous amnesia. The man on the news implied that wolves have no place among us if they gross us out by jumping on Bambi and eating him without cooking him first. This is hubris. This is silly. This is very bad biology. Face it and be awed by the true wild. The wolf on your nature poster is a killer, a predator of supreme skill and endurance. The human in your mirror is an animal. Both revelations should humble and ennoble us.

Undated

California

On a recent trip to California, I found myself stuck on a freeway. Three lanes of cars spewing exhaust, the fumes popping my few remaining brain cells like bubble wrap, nearly knocking me unconscious so that if the traffic ever did move again, I, slumped over the steering wheel, dripping stalactites of drool onto the rental car's tasteful silver carpet, would incite gridlock anew, and the other drivers, their bloodstreams raging with espresso, would hate me and start shooting.

The car ahead of me in this traffic jam was a BMW with an in-dash fax and Jacuzzi. Its bumper sticker said, "I'd rather be hunting and gathering."

Californians dine by a sacred creed that says, "Eat fresh foods produced locally." "We don't shop at supermarkets," they sniff. "We forage." And it's off to buy fetal zucchini from Buddhists, oysters shucked by the Holy Ghost, olives cured in the spittle of Himalayan puppies. Does anyone in the Golden State go hungry?

I cannot speak from experience because I grew up, and remain, well-fed. We were not a "think of starving children in China" kind of family, each meal dredged in béchamel and guilt. The Great Depression was my parents' tribal history. They understood necessity and never used hunger as punishment. They never sent us to our rooms without dinner—only without dessert.

If they served a lesson with the green beans, it was to appreciate my mother's labors. While her peers tripped over their aprons in the post-war rush to convenience foods, my mother drew on an eclectic cuisine known in our household as "from scratch." My young lips never touched orange squares of petro-cheese, smelted between two slabs of snow-white, inflatable bread.

Only as a young adult did I first see true hunger. At a city diner, I sat across the room from a shabby vagrant who was nursing a cup of coffee, the only food he could afford. When he thought no one was looking, he uncapped the bottle of ketchup set among the table condiments and drank it down like a cold beer. A vegetarian obviously.

Today's gourmet snobbery bears a curious irony. Paté and meat pies, once the fare of peasants, now melt the palates of the affluent, who scorn Spam and pre-whipped substances made with the oil-based flavors we fought Iraq for. The food elite have adopted the cuisine of the poor, but they have left the poor with the ketchup bottle.

To irony, add the illusion that we can hunt and gather, that we can live off the land and eat food close to the source. Not too many people remember what the source is. Not much of either source or land is left. Imagine everyone in Provo foraging. Imagine yourself wringing the necks of chickens or grappling with bleeding, bleating goats.

What if, like the bumper sticker said, I truly had to hunt and gather? I would see more songbird and reptile on my plate. I could clobber great blue herons and loot passing RVs. Around me lies the perfect "from scratch" cuisine: bunny linguine, baked meadowlarks, the neighbor's kittens. Eat your pets!

May 29, 1998

Cracking Up

W hat is this odd feeling in the air today? A change in the weather? Diesel fumes? Unhappy subatomic particles?

I caught the feeling when I saw an elderly woman drive a sedan the size of a cocktail lounge down the busiest one-way street in town going the wrong way. A defiant cloud of blue hair barely topped the dashboard. Her hands clutched the wheel in a death grip. She knew precisely what she was doing, as if that morning she had bolted up from her Barcalounger and said to her poodle, "Move your butt, Muffy, we're taking the Buick down Eleventh Avenue the wrong way."

Call it compulsive personal anarchy. One morning the time molecules whir in your ears, "You're nearly fifty and you still wear flannel pajamas with little red fire engines on them."

You stumble to the bathroom. You lean over the basin and stare down at the stalactite of toothpaste foam that hangs from your lips. Slowly, you lift your head and look in the mirror. A strange smile crosses your face as if you'd rather like to bite someone.

"I must have snapped or something," said Orville Wyatt Lloyd of Texas, explaining how he mistook his mother-in-law for a large raccoon and hacked her to death.

For years you bravely cope. Then one day you see phrases like "priority based interface" or "quantum near-death synchronicity" and you want to rush to a supermarket and empty a sandblaster onto every box of Count Chocula in the aisle.

Inside the market: the quietly pulsating neon tubes, the hum of distant freezers, the little cans of tomato paste. Outside the market: impending nuclear incineration, the vitriolic drone of hate radio, defense attorneys, teenagers with driver's licenses, pit bulls that could eat your face. "Lobotomy!" I screech to a friend when I'm nearly over the brink. I wonder if anyone these days just grabs their neurosurgeon by the lapels and demands a lobotomy.

My friend urges me to tune into the sounds of nature. I picture myself squinting at snowcapped peaks or staring into majestic canyons, feeling humbled and soothed. "Not necessary," he says and hands me a video and a tape of environmental noises.

In my headset, clouds whisper, birds chirp, forests murmur, dolphins gurgle. On my TV screen, sunrises glow. Slow motion ocean waves build, crest, and crash. My living room reeks of kelp. No need to die in a rip-tide or go to the Grand Canyon and suffer vertigo, heat stroke, or Gila monster bites all over your ankles. The whole ditch, every last flake of Vishnu Schist, is on a nature cassette.

When the world bears down, what counts is not a self-indulgent wallow. What counts are small acts of defiance. The true rebels against a suffocating culture of meaninglessness may be the little old ladies with Buicks.

"Move your butt," I tell my gerbil as I grab the truck keys. "We're heading for Eleventh Avenue."

June 21, 1996

Rural Realities

Tuesday is my favorite day at the post office because I can immerse myself in a vibrant world of color and human dignity. I can stand on one of the few places in the country where, on the lip of the twenty-first century, in the red rock heart of the American West, no English is spoken. As I collect my letters and among them ignore pleas from impatient friends who nag me to get e-mail, I hear around me the sounds of an Athabaskan language. Centuries ago it came from Asia across the Bering Strait, then moved down the Rocky Mountain cordillera to the southwestern deserts and stayed. Navajo is a tongue at once bitten off and as dry as a wind in a raven's wings. I revel in the act of pure listening without the burden of understanding.

On Tuesdays, a county services van collects elderly Navajos from remote parts of the reservation and brings them to town for the day. The van, filled with aged men and women, stops at the post office. When the young driver opens the door, out billows a crashing boom of radio set at top volume for poorly functioning hearing aids. Usually it's chants on the tape deck or rapid-fire Navajo on KTNN from Chinle, Arizona, heavy on the bass.

On a town day, the seniors always dress up. The men wear faded snap shirts, black Stetsons, and belts ablaze with silver and turquoise. The women's style embodies their tribe's legendary ability to adopt ideas from other cultures then ground them as essential Navajo traits. Their long fluted cotton skirts and velveteen blouses date back to Pueblo and ultimately Spanish influence. Their headscarves are pure 1950s. They wear hot pink or lime green canvas Keds with orange crew socks. They are loaded down with the family wealth of turquoise and silver jewelry.

There are no pastels here. Every color draws from the desert around us. Crimson and vermilion from sandstone cliffs lit by the sun, deep indigo from the shadows, purple and emerald from the far mesas. For a Navajo, color is not just a color, but a universe. A reflection of a profound bond between land and human.

When the elders were young they relied on a pastoral economy, raising sheep for family sustenance and trade goods. They are likely the last generation to have done so.

Today at the post office, the most important piece of mail is the Social Security check. It isn't much, but it is everything. In tough times it may have to feed ten or eleven people. Many rural Navajos live close to the edge of real hunger, but they do not see themselves as poor.

Their land ennobles them. The greatest deprivation would not be a lack of material wealth, but the loss of place.

On this Tuesday at least, life has certain compensations. It's an occasion to wear jewelry, to have a good time. The surrounding desert appears endless, filled with the most vivid colors on Earth. There is no poverty of aesthetics. If the retirement check comes in, if the family is fed, and if the van picks you up for a ride to town, today the only other wealth you need is the rich, far lost beauty of Indian country around you.

March 21, 1997

Montana

Geographers often describe Montana's size with the "how many states can fit into it" measure. Two Vermonts, nearly three Connecticuts, one slightly distended West Virginia. Montana has been called the space between people, implying that you need a vehicle and a tank of gas to bring you close enough to see if the other person's eyes are blue or brown. So much space fosters philosophy and narrative invention, desirable traits for writers, cowboys, and that up-and-coming New West prodigy, the golf pro.

Under the Western sky, comfort is found in your own insignificance. As a young insignificant woman, I believed that Montana was big enough to hold my restlessness. I thought I might find root in a place of this size. I went to Montana as a native Westerner, exchanging one outback home for another.

The growing season was so brief I had to jumpstart my garden inside a junked farm truck that sat on its axle in my backyard. The truck made a perfect greenhouse.

Its cab and windshield faced south for solar gain. Its windows adjusted for ventilation.

In Montana I survived winters of brittle, frigid air that burned the skin like poison needles. I boldly crawled under the house to thaw my pipes with a blow-dryer. When a severe cold snap froze every molecule of liquid in my house, except a tumbler of whiskey, I drank the whiskey.

In Montana I learned to row a river, belly dance, and herd sheep. I frost-nipped my feet on ski trips in moonlight. I rearranged my knees on trucks with a heavy pack. The land seemed so vast, each season so deep, adventure was irresistible. Those years matched youth to place, reckless energy to a land that does not yield easy living to anyone.

I lived in a town with a past as Western as bullet holes and a stop sign. As it outgrew its frontier motleyness, the locals wanted churches and schools. Visitors from the East wanted bugling elk and virile men who punched each other's lights out. These days los hombres de global economy dress like Garth Brooks on weekends, but demand a four-lane to the ski lift. They want cow poop on their boots and Ralph Lauren in their living rooms. Everyone wants Montana to be not a state, but a state of mind.

I have not lived in Montana for a number of years, but I know that its serious space has become serious real estate. Hoarding the limelight are a ranch-hungry Hollywood elite, golf pros, and nearly everyone from California who saw the fly-fishing movie. They visit

Montana for two days in July and exclaim, "Let's move here! The bad weather is a myth. The people are so nice." Well of course they're nice. They're not freezing to death. They're not yet stir-crazy enough to shoot their refrigerators.

Although Montana's spaces fit me well, I did not take root in northern light. Eventually I left for the desert where I always belonged, but didn't know it. The West tutors us in native migration. It tells us to look for a home that can grasp the paradox of love and complication. It helps us decide what kind of men and women we want to be.

During my Montana years, I did what we all must do to learn how to live here. I simply tucked my young and reckless life into a fold of high handsome land and I held on.

Undated

Summer

·POTSHERD·

Australia

The lapis sky and red earth of central Australia strike a native nerve. They are the colors of home in southern Utah. I want to hike across the desert but it's 118 degrees. I recall the story of an early outback explorer who could not write in his notebook because the lead in his pencil melted and dripped out the tip onto his paper.

Also, I don't want to scare goannas, Australia's version of monitor lizard. Some of them are the size of a skateboard. Out here where trees are scarce, a startled goanna will run up the highest object within reach—which is you. Male goannas have two penises. So there I would be, bone marrow oozing out of my feet like pencil lava, a frightened, two-penised goanna on my head, his anxious claws carving tiny scratches in my scalp as he twirls around to look for the danger.

We hike to a water hole and swim in liquid the color of strong tea, unperturbed by a pile of spiders on a rock. Some Australian spiders bark, others are so large they eat birds. These spiders could open their mouths and in would fly a doomed flock of crows.

Two Aborigine boys join us in the pool. Their smiles are enchanted. They speak in a soft tongue that is all cadence. Before Europeans came, Australia's Aborigines had no wheel, no writing, no pockets, no hats. They made no distinction between landscape and dreams. It's how to live in this brutal desert with complete grace.

Evening brings little relief, only black-flanked rock wallabies to stare at us, those silly little four legs hanging limp beneath their sweet chins. In the dense, Antipodean underdark, the stars emerge. The Southern Cross, Orion standing on its head, Magellanic Clouds, a Milky Way so broad with one tweak it would fall around your face like a veil. The heat does not break.

February 3, 1995

Geese

The birds of Desolation Canyon fall into three groups: year-round residents, migrants, and the seasonals that re-occupy the river corridor each spring because the air is warm and insects have emerged abundant and edible.

I find great solace in the homebodies, perhaps because of their orthodoxy, their unshakable faith in one place. What if birds had religion? Magpies would be Catholics, of course, in their black and white clerical feathers. Woodpeckers would be some kind of Holy Roller. Surely snowy egrets must be the Holy Ghost herself, brilliant white against the red rock, aloof and regal atop black legs and wacky yellow feet. If I were a sensible grey chukar, I would probably be Lutheran. If I were a resident Canada goose, in Desolation Canyon, on a rising river, I'd be nervous.

Most of our geese nest on the river's islands, ringing themselves with a mote of safety against predators. Considering such security, why would I be a nervous wreck? Because runoff and nesting periods coincide. I would pick a spot, lay a handsome clutch, then watch the river rise. How am I to know the year's snowpack or the flows released from the mega-dam upriver, driven not by nature but by bureaucrats? Such variables affect the timing and volume of high water.

I'd feel my warm eggs beneath me. I'd watch the swelling river eat my island. I'd be a spooked goose in the middle of a desert about to flood. I'd think, "Aren't Canada geese supposed to live in mountains or on mist-kissed lakes? Shouldn't they be living in Canada?"

In the Middle Ages, people believed that goose embryos developed inside mussels. The shiny, black shells clung to shoreline rocks, popped open, and out flew a flock of geese. Medieval biology was miserably wrong, but not the link between water and bird, environment and instinct. No goose can live without water.

Here in the Utah desert, the river is both a lifeline and a peril. In this year's race between incubation and high water, the geese have won. Seldom do nests flood. The eggs hatched and off waddled a fine brood of goslings, a new generation of Green River homebodies.

July 21, 1994

Bluff

Perhaps it began with the wind. For weeks, the wind blew its dry burden of red dust down the canyons and across the open desert into our ears, our pockets, our nerves. The wind lifted up the top three inches of Arizona and dropped it on our heads. The gusts made the roots of my hair ache. No one in Bluff could remember so much wind blowing day and night, day after day.

People grew testy and distracted, but we knew our land well. We knew the stillness would return, even as we longed for it. Then one day the wind did stop. The Earth tilted and Bluff slid.

After killing a policeman in nearby Colorado, three anti-government extremists surfaced east of Bluff, where one of them shot and wounded a local deputy. Within hours, the somnolent little town turned into an armed camp with roadblocks, helicopters, SWAT teams, canine tracking units, and hundreds of edgy men in uniform darting madly about with small arsenals on their persons.

Early in the manhunt, my husband Mark and I were allowed through a roadblock late at night. We drove to our isolated house above the river. Where Bluff should have been, there was a blank space, an inky darkness. The entire town had disappeared. No one told us that residents had been evacuated.

From some obscure heap of dust balls, Mark unearthed his old shotgun, put it next to our bed. The damaged gun barrel was unnervingly curved. The label on the ammunition box showed a pleasantly plump pheasant.

As a thudding fleet of choppers passed over us, Mark told me that if I had to use the gun, I should aim for the crotch. "Whose crotch?" I asked, certain that the outlaws were all at once somewhere, anywhere, everywhere. When I took a shower, it felt like the movie *Psycho*.

The Bluff school, used as a command post, swarmed with troops. The testosterone was so thick a woman could get pregnant just by walking down the hall. The map room was strangely chilly, an oasis of detumescence.

When it was discovered that we had not evacuated, that our isolated property had not been checked, and that I was alone while Mark worked, I was given two sets of advice.

A sheriff's deputy said, "Get yourself some guns."

The FBI said, "We'll give you an escort." I took the escort.

"Get guns?" I mumbled as five FBI guys led me down my driveway. "Get myself some guns?"

Obviously, I was the only person in North America without them. One token, squishy, white doughball of

liberalism who still believed that if you hated government, maybe you should do something really radical to
change things, like vote.

I wondered if arms against arms created an endless
spin into violence. I wondered why the world had turned
so vicious. I wondered why the FBI guys wore bullet-
proof vests and I did not.

They poised their rifles as we reached the house and,
with quiet courtesy, asked me for permission to enter.

I stood outside in a limp noodle posture, my wildlife
menagerie around me—lizards, rabbits, ravens, the bull
snake that napped under the mint bushes, the flycatcher
and her nest of baby birds in our eave. I looked through
the glass doors at the way too many books, my stupid
little piles of river rocks, the fetishes from Mexico, the
Navajo mud toys.

The armed search precipitated a wholesale destruc-
tion of the lyrical. It felt dreamy and unreal, like hand
grenades in a monastery.

These days, people still recount manhunt anecdotes.
They recall the endless rumors, such as the one about the
outlaws hijacking a UPS truck and terrorizing the Four
Corners region in little brown suits.

Countless stories are told, all but the most critical
one. That is, what really happened and why did these men
disrupt so many lives with their survivalist fantasy, one
that arms itself to the teeth and touts violence as a virtue?

Two of the fugitives remain at large. They will likely
surface when they become bold or miss their mommies.
Meanwhile, people in Bluff slowly reclaim the river and

de-spook their yards, trails, and canyons. I look at my neighbors' faces and see a bone-deep fatigue.

The wind has returned. It comes up every afternoon, pushing heat and dust, rattling the dry cottonwood leaves and thrashing my hair about my face. We long for stillness.

This time, no one is sure that it will come again so easily. In Bluff's deep peace, there is a severe crack.

July 24, 1998

Guests

My house is surrounded by a menagerie of wildlife. They think of us as their pets or, at best, as interesting as fence posts. They believe we built the house for them, creating shelters, stones to bask on, insects to eat, flowers to sip.

All of us, the wildlife and we fence posts, live in a peaceful state of anarchy. Hummingbirds the size of a heartbeat collide full speed into the window screens. With beaks stuck in the small squares, they madly vibrate their wings in reverse and go nowhere. I punch them out of the vice with the flat of my hand, trying not to snap off their beaks. Pheasants squawk, ravens quark, geese honk, the coyotes yip and yowl all night.

By day it rains lizards. Two spiny lizards chase and wrestle one another, scramble up a cottonwood then drop at my feet when I pass. The lizards are so inflated with reptilian machismo, you could strap one to each foot and skate off.

Someone leaves a door open and a side-blotched lizard, *Uta stansburiana*, tiptoes inside to explore the fence posts' inner sanctum. When it sees me it tries to race across the smooth clay tiles, its little lizard feet scrabbling madly in place.

A cricket takes up residence in my husband's closet. At night, it sings love songs to his hiking boots.

The toad that lives under the mint bushes plops around the breezeway, then flings itself against a window. I think it's headed for the bathtub. These creatures allow us to reside alongside them to witness their lives.

I know this for certain when a bull snake shows up. Bull snakes are harmless, cream-colored reptiles with brown markings. Behind each eye is a stroke of black like the kohl eye makeup of an Egyptian queen. This bull snake starts at the top of the breezeway stairs next to the bleached white hipbone of a cow. She slips down from the bone, her long, supple body perfectly stair-stepped along the contours of the descent. She drops her scarlet tongue into a pool of water left from a hose and she drinks. I see her cheeks inflate with each sip. I go about my business thinking about a snake that laps up water like a thirsty dog. When I return she has assumed siesta position in a lawn chair, her tail draped over the seat like a casual whip. This snake has an aura of mischief about her: not slow and sinister, but curious, oblivious to us, but not to our possibilities. The snake keeps down the mice and chases off rattlesnakes. The bug-eating birds and lizards are cheaper, safer, and more fun than insecticides.

Hummingbirds invite me to fill our lives with flowers. Toads reassure us that there is a lot of sex going on. We think of our domestic wildlife as useful. I don't know what they think of us, but I know that they, not we, are the hosts on this shaggy piece of desert.

One day I chased two *Uta*s out of my living room. It isn't easy herding lizards. One night, outside, a tiny bat hooks itself high in the stucco wall to rest. I stand on my head to better observe this upside-down winged mouse. When you're a guest, you adjust.

Undated

Navajo Fair

A curving reef of slickrock holds the rodeo arena in its cusp, its base afloat on a hovering stratum of red dust. The dust lasts as long as Navajo Fair, three days, and friends joke that I, one of a few Anglos and as exotic as an alpaca in a sea of obsidian hair, will turn as red as their clan sisters.

Cowboys—Indians, that is—lean on the rails of a holding pen, admiring Brahma bulls. In Navajo, the rodeo announcer reels out a play-by-play of the chicken pull, his commentary sprinkled with "Southern fried" and "discount prices." Some English simply does not translate. Freckles, for instance. There is no Navajo word for freckles.

Chicken pulls go back many years. A chicken was buried up to its neck in dirt. One by one, horsemen passed at a run, leaning over to yank the bird out of the hole. These days, chickens are burlap sacks of prize money. When a rider from Teec Nos Pos grabs the sack without falling off his horse, the crowd cheers.

At fair time, people come from the surrounding desert to gossip and joke with old friends. When my group tackles a serious subject in Navajo, I ask a friend to translate. No one cracks a smile until he turns to me and says, "They're planning to get three boats and invade Spain."

Fair day ends with a heartbeat of drums and a blur of feathers as dancers whirl beneath a brush ramada. The drummers pitch their songs to a crescent moon, their voices an eerie mix of wind, wolf, and shriek. Sunset drenches the slickrock in bloodred light, and the air fills with juniper smoke from cooking fires.

Late into the night, The Wind Singers, a women's drum group, close the powwow with a social dance. Dancers and audience participate, but since they appear reluctant, the announcer gives them a nudge. "The Wind Singers are sitting all alone up here, waiting for you men to dance with them," he says. "They're all good looking. They have lots of money and really nice cars."

August 8, 1997

Lawn

In Utah, God wants you to have a lawn. An unkempt, weedy yard around a house can mean only one thing: the person inside is dead.

Where I live is an anomaly. There are few formal lawns. The church, school, and several homes sit on rectangles of green chives that appear to be groomed by fleets of young cyborgs in green jumpsuits wielding tiny, busy scissors.

Everyone else wrangles an intifada of motley weeds. People nurture shade trees, drought-tolerant flowers, perhaps a tomato patch and some wicked chiles destined for a conflagrational salsa.

A lawn is based on the principle of overcoming rather than adapting to local conditions. Here, lawnlessness is not a shirking of one's religious duty to conquer bestial nature—it is adaptive realism.

I look at my own eight-acre desert plot as a kind of slob's Walden Pond. It retains its unruly character by sheer defiance and lovable perversity. The aesthetics come not from a vanity afforded by wetter climates but from the narrower margins of aridity. I am not its gardener but an avocational meddler. Sometimes, the weeds are so furiously aggressive I'm tempted to stand back and see what happens next. Who will usurp who? Which of those isolated tufts of puny leaves actually has roots clear into New Mexico? Is it true that tumbleweeds can germinate in thirty-six minutes?

On our land, we grow vegetables, herbs, and wildflowers. My husband talks of planting a small rectangle of grass under his lawn chair. Otherwise, there is no possibility of a lawn. We do not own a lawn mower, but we do have principles. Quite frankly, this is the definition of a lawn: throw massive amounts of water and petrochemicals on your grassy plot, let it push up from the soil, then cut it down to nubs before it can grow up and have sex and go to seed. A lawn is an endless cycle of doomed ecology.

I may claim that lawns are out of place in the desert. I may call myself an adaptive realist. But without a dense crew cut of green, I am likely some sort of unsmelted, botanically derelict communist. And surely, in the eyes of a lawn-loving God, hell-bound.

September 4, 1998

West Virginia

S ometimes the best way to know the West is to leave it. In summer I accepted an invitation to a conference in West Virginia. I packed the essentials—jungle clothes, dictionary, duct tape—and flew east on one of Delta's flying culverts. Clouds covered the land below the airplane. I had no idea what was underneath me beyond the generality North America. To be without defining topography unnerves me. Before I arrived, I was already lost.

The conference venue was surrounded by a dense hardwood forest. I felt homesick for the dry, wide-open red rock desert of my southern Utah home. In West Virginia, the sky rested at about ear level. I could not find a horizon that felt true, that did not shimmer or shift shape in the aquarium air. I learned that the light itself bore weight. I learned that I would not get far if I called a hollow an arroyo.

The best way to understand a strange place is by local knowledge. I don't mean museum history or a litany of factoids or the cosmic metaphors in a zip code. I mean the lay of the land and the stories that describe it. You must be alert to the contours that make the place somewhere, not just anywhere. Don't carry a map to the mall, carry a bird book. If there are neither birds nor books you've learned a telling feature of the place. Find a toehold. Slow down. Pay attention. Go deep. Ask why people call their landscape home, what they love or fear, what is blessed, what is destroyed.

In my desert home, the key piece of local knowledge is water: carrying it, finding it, knowing it. In a country where water hurls through canyons or strains against a necklace of dams, rivers tell everything you need to know about this land and its people. When I travel to a new place, the first thing I do is seek the nearest water. Through the window of river lies a path to the true stories of place.

In West Virginia I found the Potomac, a river dark with tannin, embraced by a thick canopy of trees. I glommed onto a friendly Easterner like a leech and I thrashed my way through the forest he called "the woods." I was ready to trek down any hollow he led me. I confessed my horizon problem. "I can't see very far around here," I said as we walked. "Everything is middle distance."

In the thick forest and humid air, I felt lost inside a giant green marshmallow. I did not need my desert squint. The lope of my native Western stride had me banging my forehead on a tree branch in a single step.

As we sat by the river, my guide told me, "The old folks around here fear the woods even as they live in them and use them and love them. In fact, for older generations, this is a terrifying place."

His words felt like a gem thrown at my feet. They offered a rich vein of place stories to be mined. They were my opening line to local knowledge. To earn this unfamiliar world, its darkness and its light, I had to follow the contours: slow down, pay attention, stay local, go deep. East, west, or in-between, relation to the land is the core of home.

Undated

Fall

·PINYON CONE·

Bighorn Sheep

Six bighorn sheep feed across the river from me. I did not seek them out. They came to me. We are spending the day together.

The sheep band is all ewes and lambs with gentle faces and white bands down slender legs as smooth as smoke. The dominant ewe has a chocolate-brown face, a scar on her flank, and no lamb. Another ewe is lighter brown and younger. Her lamb is half sleek fur, half baby fluff, giving the impression of a bursting cattail.

Their agility on the ever-crumbling canyon walls takes your breath away. Their bodies are all springs and coils, shock absorbers and cushions of muscle and sinew. They cling to the thinnest, sheerest ledge as if with Velcro.

The ewes feed quietly on the riverbank, aware of me but showing no sign of alarm. Heads tilted, amber-gold eyes soft and curious, they follow my stroll up and down the beach like lobs at a tennis game. I eat my sandwich. They eat their greens. I sit down. They retire to a ledge high on the cliff, chewing. When they rest, I rest. The ewes tuck their babies behind them against the wall, taking the side with the sheer drop.

After our nap, the bighorns rise to their feet and leave the ledge. They trot resolutely downriver in single file as if they had a dentist appointment in Grand Junction.

When they disappear, the afternoon feels empty. I grew accustomed to their strange eyes with horizontal irises, the sheep look that says, "Come closer so I can chew off your buttons."

If you look for bighorn sheep, you won't find them. Even hard-rock patience usually ends in disappointment. Bighorns are so elusive in this canyon, so invisible, it's as if they live inside seams of time. Yet in the coming weeks, I will see this same band often. Our paths will cross without my seeking them. I simply fall into their seam of remoteness and serenity.

September 15, 1995

Tourists in the Wild

At dusk in a tourist village in Yellowstone Park, a sleek Continental stops me as I cross the road. It is the color of zinfandel grapes. It has New York plates. A tinted window hums down. "Which way to West Yellowstone?" asks the driver, a harried man who looks like a bowling pin.

His companions bear the same edge of panic and bowling pin shape. All three are frazzled, as if they had driven all the way from Brooklyn without stopping and suddenly found themselves in the backhoe capital of the world where large, poorly fed mammals could easily squeeze them through the taillights of their Continental like toothpaste through a tube.

When I explain that they have missed their turn by fifty miles, their looks go from frazzled to crazed. They must find West Yellowstone, they wail. They have a hotel reservation there. Are there any other hotels in Montana? They peer furtively out the windows into the darkness. I think it best not to mention that they're actually in Wyoming.

I recommend the hotel across the way, pointing to a dim glow of light. Not a great distance, but one of the women shrieks and clutches my arm as if I had suggested she rub bacon grease all over her body, leap through the bison poop, and head for a well-known grizzly habitat.

The words "parking lot" are the first familiar words I utter to them, but it gets them the next few yards, where they wedge their cruiser next to an RV topped by a satellite dish big enough to chum in a stealth bomber.

Getting the trio out of the car isn't easy. Before they emerge, they stuff guidebooks, maps, mosquito netting, first aid kits, lunch, and a giant canister of insect repellent into a canvas tote bag.

They take deep breaths and emerge from the car. I lead them to the hotel entrance, their bodies glued to me like segments on an ant. We arrive inside without a single bear attack. I wave goodbye at the lobby door.

Left alone in the mountain darkness, I feel no terror, but I understand theirs. It is exactly how I would feel if I were lost at night in Brooklyn.

October 3, 1997

Toads

If you are a toad in the desert, nature has designed a simple strategy for reproducing yourself. It rains, you sing, you copulate—very quickly.

The lives of desert toads hang on opportunity. Rain, the desert's most unpredictable element, cues their lust, and when it does, the toads emerge from their sandy burrows to find mates scattered across the land like long-lost golf balls. For this, they need robust voices.

A stout drum of male toad flesh sets off sound waves that reach the ear of a female, who will love him or dump him for his song. Toads in open deserts have more audible calls than forest dwellers. Their voices carry across long distances of clear, dry air. Older toads have greater bass than smaller, squeaky teenage toads. A cold toad produces a slower, lower-pitched call than a warm one. Depending on species, toad voices can resemble sheep bleats, creaky doors, squashed ducks, a berserk handsaw, or a pencil stroking the teeth of a comb.

Most of my neighborhood toads are bufos, the true toads, and spadefoots, named for the digging phalanges on their hind feet. They bear little resemblance to the svelte, smooth-skinned, shiny, moist frog cousins that live among leaves or near permanent water. Spadefoot and bufo bodies look like pudgy, gray-brown dirigibles.

You can, but shouldn't, carry them around in your hands like a pork chop. When you think about licking them, change your mind. Some species secrete skin chemicals that cause discomfort, sneezing, illness, or hallucinations, all of which add up to an ingenious defense against any predator that wraps its jaws around what appears to be a plump lunch. Using its skin as a weapon, the toad might hunker down in "eat me" position rather than leap away from danger.

Classical violinists in Europe handled a toad before a performance so that the toad's neurotoxins might paralyze the secretion glands in their hands and prevent sweaty palms.

Navajo toad stories describe an unruly animal spirit with swollen eyes and rough body bumps that he claims are potatoes. When he attends ceremonies, he brings his messy grandchildren, who swarm all over the place and wet the floor where people must sit.

Some of us fight an urge to interfere with toads, to handle creatures so perfectly born of rain, air, and canyon, yet we can only earn their mystery when they come within voyeur's reach and we let them slip away.

Try this: after a summer monsoon, share camp with a colony of sex-crazed bufos. You have one precious instant to fix them in your gaze, to taste their stolid, amphibian wisdom, the ancient imperative to unbury themselves from the sand, to sing and mate.

Piggybacked in their copulation embrace, they move in a series of muscular hurls followed by squishy, rubber-bag plops. If you really must know, the male is on top. Try to give them privacy by looking the other way. It isn't easy.

October 17, 1997

The Dump

The days of my town dump are numbered. It's a deep-pit, landfill-style dump surrounded by a thousand acres of open desert with a view well into the next state. You can spot the dump by a plume of smoke or a scattered confetti of jet-black ravens and airborne bits of paper and plastic.

The county will soon replace our dump with a transfer station. Instead of dirtballing across the sand with our motley loads, we will drive up a tidy gravel ramp that leads to a tidy row of dumpsters into which we will drop our tidy bundles of garbage. When the dumpsters are full, trucks will haul them to a landfill to the north, also in the middle of the desert with ravens and plastic and a million-dollar view. For a fee, this dump will collect any dead animals we happen to discard. Ten dollars for a dead horse, two bucks fifty for a sheep.

The old dump is a mess. Most of us are quite fond of it, especially now that it is destined to be a mess no longer. Gusty winds blow plastic sacks all over the desert, where they have not quite begun to biodegrade.

The old dump is always on fire. The smoke rises thick and black behind the "no burning allowed" sign. On quiet days, a heap of charred cans smolders in the pit. You park, walk a minefield of diapers, then pass mattresses exploding their inner fluff, hulks of old washing machines, and a large, possibly toxic sofa. You resist the pathetic hungry puppy that some jerk abandoned here. You also resist taking a peek at the address labels on the mail-order sex magazines strewn among the yellow plastic Pennzoil bottles, because you really don't care to know which of your neighbors subscribes to such things.

Then you edge up to the lip of the fiery pit and test the heat. If your Tevas melt, it's probably not a good day to scavenge.

Because we live many miles from the nearest store, people around here save and reuse nearly everything. When we finally haul something to the dump, we're not convinced that its life has truly ended. By unspoken agreement, we segregate our ambivalence. Sure stuff, like kitchen garbage, goes onto the pyre. Furniture, appliances, and scrap lumber are set aside so the next person can look them over, perhaps remove some screws or nails or recycle a wire or turn a chair leg into a stake for a tomato plant.

No one knows when we will change from the old dump to the new system. When the change comes, there will no longer be an ambivalence heap. We will have to bite the bullet. We will have to drive to New Mexico for our screws. No one will miss the flaming pyre, and when the wind blows, no one will miss the plastic stuck all over the greasewood. We shall see the end of polite scavenging. We will never know who bought a new sofa and cast out the old, who gutshot their TV, or who gets the sex stuff. When the old dump closes, when the debris of our lives falls into the chasm of a tidy steel box behind a chain-link fence, we shall know a lot less about one another.

October 25, 1996

Sick of Election

The nightly news dumps an avalanche of misery and terror into my living room but says nothing about how I am to endure it. When Bob Dole comes on, I shove a plug into a socket and roar the vacuum cleaner up and down the floor in berserk stripes—all the better if I pick up an angry clatter of screws and as many hairballs as I can possibly suck up. Bill Clinton gets the blender stuffed with forks set on a slow frappé escalated to liquefy.

When I vow to dismiss any politician who cannot pronounce "nuclear," I'm left with no one to vote for. "Nucular," say the people to whom we have entrusted the primary death anxiety of the rest of history. "Let's go for the nucular."

What has become of the honorable and decent public servant? You won't find one in either political party, so kill your television.

Snagged on a reef of intolerance and self-interest, we look for heroes in the wrong places. We ought to admire people who make something creative out of their lives but don't care if anyone else knows about it. We need people who refuse to go through life as doorknobs. We need eccentrics.

As soon as I begin my research, the mentors surface. An elderly Italian feels compelled to live on trains no matter where they are going. A Scotswoman offers herself as a virgin sacrifice atop an extinct volcano in Edinburgh. Disguised as a pink elephant, an office worker scales tall buildings. An Irishman cites biblical precedent for using his maid as a hot-water bottle. In Montana, a bachelor rancher strapped by depressed cattle prices raises cash by designing women's lingerie.

My personal favorite is Oofty Goofty, a nineteenth-century San Francisco street person who turned his high threshold for pain into an asset. Oofty Goofty made his living by having people club him with a two-by-four.

Genuine eccentrics hardly know who they are. "The world they look out at is too gray for them," wrote novelist William Trevor. The peculiarities that come to govern their lives may even keep certifiable insanity at bay. Often they merely fear boredom.

Seldom do true eccentrics run for political office, probably because governing ceased to be innovative around July of 1776. Instead, the Edinburgh virgin, the train fetishist, the underwear rancher, and others live within the confines of their own adventures. Outlandish but private, their acts endanger only themselves.

Such harmless creativity would do us a world of good as we numbly tune in election ads or mindless video battles with assault weapons, detecting absolutely no difference between them.

My television is dead. The vacuum cleaner and blender lie idle, but, as a precaution, my husband has hidden his chainsaw. I'm certain that the piranhas chumming for my vote cannot penetrate. And thus I wade through a glory of eccentrics, grateful that somewhere out there, a few people have the courage to keep insanity at bay.

November 1, 1996

Season Wrap Up

For thousands of days, my life has been ruled by the Green River—by its flow and the distance it takes me each day, by its speed and volume, its ever-changing light.

This morning, the river is noisy with the rapid near camp. It is red, not from sediment, but from the reflection of salmon-red canyon walls on the water.

Raft loaded, we shove off the gravel bar and pinball across the rocky shallows into the current. Low water requires work. The raft floor barely skims over shallow bars like the one called Deviated Septum Riffle. I named it when an oar blade struck bottom and propelled the shaft like a spear into my nose. It was a painful lesson about rowing too deeply.

Above rapids, I cannot see the runs through the dazzling glare of low-slung sun that splinters the river's surface into blinding fragments. At this low volume, the rocks are meaner. Some runs require threading-the-needle maneuvers and a folding in of oars to avoid smashing them into a maze of exposed boulders.

After living in Desolation Canyon for six months, twenty days a month with oars in my fists, the river's muscle shows itself in my arms and back and in calluses so thick winter's respite won't be long enough to soften them. My hands will be ready to take the oars next spring without blistering. Sun and papery dry air have mapped themselves on our hides. Tenderness lives in the lines at the corners of my husband's eyes. When I stand against the sandstone, he says, there is no difference between me and the red-gold canyon. I have turned the color of Desolation.

October 13, 1995

Winter

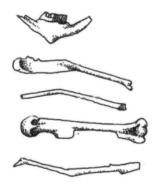

· BONES OF A SMALL MAMMAL ·

Moose

Each winter a moose appears to me. I do not seek this moose. It simply manages to be there. An appearing moose lacks the fleeting uncertainty of the typical wildlife sighting. My moose is never a blur. It usually stands at the edge of a swamp as if it had been there forever. A fur-covered coat rack embedded in cement. And I just happen to swing by while it's stuck. This gives me plenty of time to study its dangly dewlap. Those droopy lips. The pendulous muzzle plastered with swamp turf. That bony mass sticking out of its head like a wordless cartoon bubble.

Perhaps the moose is trying to think. Poet Ted Hughes says moose are like this because they can't find the world.

"Where is the world?" the moose groans. "Oh my lost world. And why am I so ugly? And why am I so far away from my feet?"

Someone else said that moose always look as if they are suffering for theories that no one else agrees with.

Somewhere out there lives the flat-Earth moose and the cold-fusion moose.

I spot this year's thinking moose, a bull, at the edge of an aspen grove in Yellowstone National Park. He stands very still, looking as if he could level two hefty aspens if he moved his head to either side. Perhaps he is waiting for his antlers to drop off before he ambles on. Perhaps he's thinking about moving to Yelverton, Canada.

Perhaps he's thankful there's snow so he doesn't have to deal with low-lying plants. Because they have short necks and towering legs, moose must spread their feet outwards or get down on their knees to eat ground vegetation. A Yellowstone moose would rather die than have a passing tourist see him kneeling. This bull remains immobile out of self-respect. All he wants is some privacy. I move on. I love moose. The dopier the better.

November 3, 1995

The Snakes in Desolation Canyon

ummer's heat has lost its ferocity. Fall slips into
shadows that border the river. Perhaps the change
of season makes everyone move. Moving creatures
make meals. This week we saw the hunger.

Whatever killed the first snake disappeared as we
arrived. The kill was fresh. A yellow-green garter snake
still silky and limp. Mark says the puncture wounds in
its scutes are from teeth. "No," I say, "talons made those
wounds." We looked for bobcat or cougar tracks but we
found none.

Around here, snakes do drop out of the sky. We often
see golden eagles flying about Desolation with snakes
dangling from their talons. Apparently a bird once
dropped a rattlesnake into a raft out of which the rafters
promptly jumped. Deliberate eagle mischief, I'm sure.

At the scene of the second dead snake, there was no
snake, but the drama unfolded clearly in the pale sand.

From one direction came elegant *S*-curve tracks. From the other, prints of a coyote in stalking gait. At their juncture, an imprint of coyote haunches, an arc of track-less air, then the deep furrows of forepaws as the coyote pounced on the snake. No body, no blood. Just lunch.

The third dead snake laid evolution at our feet. Here by the river the race between predator and prey to gain an edge ended in stalemate. The snake had swallowed a catfish. Then the fish moved or maybe the snake gagged. The catfish flared its gills, and like those tire spikes that let cars out of an exit but not in without ugly shredding, the spines on the fish's gills caught in the snake's throat. The snake choked. The fish died for lack of water. Evolutionary stalemate.

For a fourth snake it was not a bad week at all. In a thatch of greasewood bushes, we saw a rabbit dragging an unusually long tail. A bull snake had her by the butt like a bulldog on a sofa. The snake let go and swallowed a mouthful of fur. Then it swallowed one or two of the baby bunnies in a nearby nest. The mother rabbit approached. The snake again clamped jaws on her tail. While the rabbit hopped about with a snake attached to her rear end, the magpies helped themselves to bunny parts. No blood, no guts. Just lunch.

November 11, 1994

Bread Dough

The bread dough contains too much leavening, but I punch it down and cover the bowl. I put it on the floor of the truck cab to transport it and other supplies out of town for the weekend.

After one quick errand at the hardware store, I note that the dough has doubled in size. Then, during a stop for groceries, it oozes down the sides of the bowl like anemic lava. I try to knead it into obedience. Pieces of dough stick to my fingers, the steering wheel, and door handles. I pray that no one is watching this drama. The headlines will read, "Godzilla's brain regenerates inside Toyota." Or, in the tabloids, "Woman sucked into massive doughball sees Elvis." The story will quote a panel of stolid homemakers who blame me for being in a parking lot instead of at home. "She used too much yeast," they will snip.

I start to cruise down the interstate. The dough rises over the bowl again. It edges towards my feet. The road is thick with highway patrol cars. I can't remember if the speed limit is fifty-five or sixty-five, as if it matters—me with my tennis shoes welded to the accelerator by five pounds of uncooked but chemically active whole wheat.

"Well, officer," I'll say if I'm stopped, "I'm just hauling Godzilla's brain down to the lab in Green River." The patrolman will look at the pulsating mass smeared all over my sneakers. He'll see the gooey blobs dripping from the gear shift. He'll notice the fifty dogs who have trailed my bumper for the entire trip, drooling. Then he'll write up a seventy-dollar ticket. He'll hand it to me and quip, "You used too much yeast."

December 8, 1995

$\mathcal{S}heep$

With the help of two dogs and a Walkman playing Mozart, I moved 750 sheep across rolling prairie to a coulee where they can drink water. They're not very good at doing this by themselves, even when they're thirsty.

The sheepdog holds the herd in a compact mass by encircling it entirely, even as the sheep lope forward. Picture this: a table of wool with three thousand legs undulating over the prairie to an exuberance of violins. It's the only way to herd sheep.

At the moment, the sheepdog is the only useful dog. His instinct is irrepressible. Off duty, he herds the ranch kids. The second dog, a Great Pyrenees, stays with the sheep all her life, day and night. She is huge. When I first met her, she trotted over to the high-clearance farm truck, jumped up, and peered into the window at me. If the window had been open, her front paws would have rested in my eye sockets. She's sweet, and she can pulverize a coyote in fourteen seconds.

A more experienced herder pushes his band of sheep to the same coulee. He is an old fellow. Off duty, he drives a clunker sedan that sounds as if dead pedestrians were stuffed up the muffler. Each morning he performs the same ritual. Ewes quietly surround his sheep wagon. He throws open the door, rubs his union suit, and pretends he doesn't see them. Then he roars over their heads, "Where's my girls?" and laughs like a maniac.

After we unite our bands at the coulee, he stays with the herd while I transport four sheep hogtied in the back of the truck. Slowly I drive cross-country on dirt clods and wheat stubble. The sheep bounce around the truck bed like berserk piñatas. They're bound for the slaughterhouse. I plug in Mozart, not in the headset but in the tape deck so my cargo can hear. It's the least I can do.

December 16, 1994

Ice Fishing

I go ice fishing for the first time. I stretch out on a
lawn chair in the middle of a frozen lake, don sun-
glasses and Walkman, and open a book. I guess this
is how you ice fish.

My husband runs frantically from hole to hole
screaming about the fish pulling his lines, but I pay no
attention. I suspect that today is the very day spring will
make a teasing debut. I believe that unless certain rituals
are performed very carefully, spring might not arrive.

Nearby, three men in full-body camouflage stare in-
tently into a dark hole in the lake as if they expect a fish
to leap out and bash its brains on the ice. Each time the
men move away from the hole, they line up in single file,
crouch slightly, and trot forward. The confident bob of three
skull-hugging crew cuts tells me that they think they're
invisible, but against the blinding winter-white landscape, their lush green jungle fatigues stand out like kelp.

Another angler wanders over to our fishing spot.
He chats about trout. Everything he says is untrue.

"Trout are bottom feeders," he proclaims. "They molt this month."

I'm too preoccupied to respond to this nonsense. I am thinking that ancient peoples engaged in elaborate dramas to keep winter on its seasonal course. They believed that unless they did so, the world would remain forever in night and ice.

We have now rounded winter's bend. Today's bright sunlight could be spring's first tease. The camouflage trio trots about as if the frozen lake were a boot camp in Guatemala. "Trout lips are inedible," rambles the chatty fisherman. "You have to cut them off."

Spring is challenging winter's bite, but it's a weak and precarious spring. A grave and holy vigilance must be maintained. And here I am stuck on the ice with survivalists and fishermen's lies.

March 15, 1996

Peculiar Home

My Navajo neighbors define home by a circle of four mountains. Boundaries mark my homeland too. I've drawn no map, but I know by instinct if I'm inside or out. Outside, my senses dull. Inside, the only difference between the desert and me is a membrane of skin. So, the first meaning of being Utahn is the slick rock beneath my heartbeat as I lie facedown on Utah itself.

Understand my setting: a tiny town in a land that looks like red bones. Being Utahn means the San Juan River at my feet, a neighbor who grows the best chiles in the world, another who grows the best melons in the universe.

I inhabit a place where there's not much chance of being eaten by large mammals. Where, thank God, the possibility of a golf course is slim. Where I must drive seventy miles to another state to buy a nail. Where, when I get to that other state, go to a liquor store, stand before a fantastic selection of wine, and start to sob, the owner says with pity, "You're from Utah, aren't you?"

Here we watch other towns go berserk with growth, then we hang on for dear life to what we love about our place. We keep this town a bit uncomfortable. We send people seventy miles to buy a nail. Life unfolds in a landscape so beautiful it makes me ache. I surrender to a nature more feral than civilized and don't care I'm this way, because everyone else here is eccentric too and wouldn't give a hoot if you wore your pajamas to the post office.

My peculiar home within greater peculiar Utah is not typical, but it's allowed—and that gives life here so much meaning.

Undated

End of Season

· POTSHERD ·

We come to Rainbow Bridge down an arduous desert trail from the Navajo mountainside. The other approach to this popular landmark is much less work. You ride a boat across Lake Powell, the reservoir atop the Colorado River, then you walk a paved path from the dock and behold the soaring ribbon of sandstone called Rainbow Bridge.

Travelers from both routes meet here. You can tell who is who. We are not the ones with the cellular phones. The tour-boat people are tidy and refreshed. Despite the long hike, my companion retains his quiet grace, as Navajos do, under dust and sweat. Frankly, I look like I've become one with a yucca plant.

The hike was a cheap piece of procrastination. It immediately followed a rafting trip, the final of many river trips I took as a seasonal ranger on a tributary east of Lake Powell. As a rite of severance from river life, I extended the season with this overland hike. Some re-enter civilization slowly, savoring their journeys. I go from sanctuary to techno shriek in head-on collision. Lunging from one extreme to the other eases the pain.

Rainbow Bridge is civilized indeed. Never have I seen so much pantyhose on the north flank of Navajo Mountain. My friend and I sit on a rock nursing blisters, pouring red sand out of our boots, plucking rattlesnakes off our ankles.

I am so hungry I could belly up to a grand buffet then eat the napkins and suck the gravy stains out of the tablecloth. After I gulp down my lunch and half my companion's, I scan the premises for hunting-gathering potential. I suffer this feral hunger whenever I come off the river.

I cannot exist in Canyon Country unless I take it into myself and discover it on my very breath. All longing converges on a single piece of geography, my red rock desert home.

As I'm poised to hack up and eat several ravens with my Swiss Army knife, my friend makes a simple observation. My appetite, he speculates, symbolizes a desire to consume the landscape before I'm torn away from it. There's nothing more impressive than a Freudian Navajo.

We meet our shuttle boat out of Rainbow Bridge and motor to the head of the lake where a sunlit ribbon of Colorado River spills into it. On the highway headed out, I crane my neck to keep the river in view until the last curve obliterates it. I turn and face the road. I'm no longer hungry. Already I'm dying of starvation.

November 22, 1996

About Ellen Meloy

Ellen Meloy was a native of the West and lived in California, Montana, and Utah. Her book *Eating Stone: Imagination and the Loss of the Wild* (2005) was a National Book Critics Circle Award finalist for nonfiction. *The Anthropology of Turquoise: Reflections on Desert, Sea, Stone, and Sky* (2002) was a finalist for the Pulitzer Prize and won the Utah Book Award and the Banff Mountain Book Festival Award in the adventure and travel category. She is also the author of *Raven's Exile: A Season on the Green River* (1994) and *The Last Cheater's Waltz: Beauty and Violence in the Desert Southwest* (2001). Meloy spent most of her life in wild, remote places; at the time of her sudden death in November 2004 (three months after completing *Eating Stone*), she and her husband were living in southern Utah.

Torrey House Press

Voices for the Land

The economy is a wholly owned subsidiary of the environment, not the other way around.

—Senator Gaylord Nelson, founder of Earth Day

Torrey House Press is an independent nonprofit publisher promoting environmental conservation through literature. We believe that culture is changed through conversation and that lively, contemporary literature is the cutting edge of social change. We strive to identify exceptional writers, nurture their work, and engage the widest possible audience; to publish diverse voices with transformative stories that illuminate important facets of our ever-changing planet; to develop literary resources for the conservation movement, educating and entertaining readers, inspiring action.

Visit www.torreyhouse.org for reading group discussion guides, author interviews, and more.

As a 501(c)(3) nonprofit publisher, our work is made possible by the generous donations of readers like you. Join the Torrey House Press family and give today at www.torreyhouse.org/give.

This book was made possible with grants from Utah Humanities, Utah Division of Arts & Museums, Jeffrey S. and Helen H. Cardon Foundation, Barker Foundation, and Salt Lake County Zoo, Arts & Parks; donations from ATL Technology, Wasatch Advisors, BookBar, The King's English Bookshop, Jeff and Heather Adams, Robert and Camille Bailey Aagard, Curt and Nora Nichols, and Paula and Gary Evershed; generous donations from valued individual donors and subscribers; and support from the Torrey House Press board of directors.

Thank you for supporting Torrey House Press.